CRAFTS
OF THE ANCIENT WORLD

THE CRAFTS AND CULTURE OF
THE AZTECS

Joann Jovinelly and Jason Netelkos

To Jessica

Published in 2002 by The Rosen Publishing Group, Inc.
29 East 21st Street, New York, NY 10010

First Edition

Library of Congress Cataloging-in-Publication Data

Jovinelly, Joann.
The crafts and culture of the Aztecs / Joann Jovinelly and Jason Netelkos.
p. cm. — (Crafts of the ancient world)
Includes bibliographical references and index.
Summary: Describes easy-to-make crafts that replicate the arts of the ancient Aztecs. Includes historical material, a timeline, a glossary, and resources.
ISBN 0-8239-3512-4 (lib. bdg.)
1. Handicraft—Mexico—Juvenile literature. 2. Aztecs—Social life and customs—Juvenile literature. 3. Mexico—History—To 1519—Juvenile literature. [1. Handicraft. 2. Aztecs—Social life and customs.] I. Title. II. Series
TT28 .J68 2002
972'.018—dc21
                                                            2001004718

Manufactured in the United States of America

Note to Parents
Some of these projects require tools or materials that can be dangerous if used improperly. Adult supervision will be necessary when projects require the use of a craft knife, an oven, a stovetop, plaster of paris, or pins and needles. Before starting any of the projects in this book, you may want to cover your work area with newspaper or plastic. In addition, we recommend using a piece of thick cardboard to protect surfaces while cutting with craft or mat knives. Parents, we encourage you to discuss safety with your children and note in advance which projects may require your supervision.

CONTENTS

THE CULTURE

Long before Europeans began to colonize parts of North America, people of Asian descent lived on Mesoamerica, the small area of land that lay between North and South America on the Gulf of Mexico. This land, now called Mexico, was a highly developed area and was known as Mexica to the people who lived there. It was home to a civilization that historians have named the Aztec Empire.

Before the Aztecs, other Mesoamericans had settled the same territory, a harsh mountainous region with areas of swampy, fertile farmlands that stretches to the coast of South America. These civilizations were the Olmecs, the Toltecs, the Mixtecs, the Zapotecs, the Maya, and the Inca. Archaeological evidence now shows that these civilizations borrowed much of their culture and beliefs from one another.

This image depicts the founding of Tenochtitlán by the Aztecs.

The people of Mexica developed certain traits and skills that contributed to the rich cultural heritage of the Aztec Empire. The Toltecs (AD 900–1187), like the Maya (1000 BC–AD 1697) before them, are considered very skilled architects. They developed sophisticated methods of building very large temples, some of which still exist today. The Zapotecs (600 BC–AD 800) were excellent artisans who could make beautiful crafts from feathers, while the Mixtecs (AD 700–1525) were known for their pottery-making skills. A written language based on pictures and symbols, known as glyphs, was first developed by the Olmecs (1200–200 BC), an advanced civilization of people who lived during a time that archaeologists call the Preclassic period. The Olmecs offered a body of knowledge to the civilizations that followed them, including

This is an illustration of Tenochtitlán, the capital of the Aztec Empire.

an agricultural system that produced a surplus of food and a calendar that recorded time, seasons, and important events. The Olmecs also developed a system of bartering, or trading, that the later Mesoamerican civilizations that came after them would adopt.

The Aztecs were not native to the land they inhabited. They began as Chichimecs, nomadic people who searched for more fertile lands when drought and famine forced them to migrate. According to legend, the Aztecs came from a place called Aztlan, somewhere in northern or northwestern Mexico, and traveled for years through desert lands, carrying with them a statue of their sun god, Huitzilopochtli. This journey probably began around AD 1200. When they finally did settle, they chose an island in the middle of Lake Texcoco, in Mexico's central basin, around AD 1325. It was there that they built their first temples and primitive shelters made with mud bricks and thatched roofs.

As the Aztecs flourished, they built one of the largest and most beautiful cities in the ancient world, Tenochtitlán (the site of modern-day Mexico City). At its height, the city spread across more than twenty miles and was home to more than 250,000 people. Within a span of only 200 years, the former nomads controlled a vast territory—the Aztec Empire—that stretched across Mexico from the Atlantic to the Pacific Oceans. This empire came to an end when the Spanish invaded Tenochtitlán in 1520, took the great Aztec ruler Montezuma hostage, and convinced him to urge the Aztecs to surrender. For his efforts, Montezuma was stoned to death by his own people. The Spanish were briefly driven out of the city, but they returned in 1521 and destroyed Tenochtitlán. The empire fell soon after.

Aztec warriors battle the Spanish invaders. Notice the clothing of feathers and animal skins and the animal-head helmet.

DAILY LIFE

The Aztecs had a rigid and structured society that was governed by kings and other nobility, priests, and warriors who served their rules. One of the most famous of these rulers was Emperor Montezuma II. When an Aztec king died, a new male ruler would be chosen from his family to serve in his place.

The most important person after a king was called a *cihuacoatl*, or "Woman Snake," another male leader who was in charge of collecting taxes, keeping important documents, and serving as chief advisor to the king. In Aztec mythology, Cihuacoatl was a goddess whose roaring signalled war. She was often pictured with a broom, signifying the sweeping away of chaos and the reintroduction of order.

The king received assistance and advice from the Council of Four, an advisory group made up of noblemen. A *tlatocan*—a larger judicial council of twelve or thirteen men—worked for the king by writing and interpreting laws and assisting Aztec warriors who maintained order in the city. Each city-state had a system of justice to punish those who disobeyed Aztec laws or who could not pay their tribute (tax) to the king. Depending on the crime, punishments ranged from shaving the head—considered a mark of great shame—to death.

Nobles lived in the center of the city of Tenochtitlán, while common people lived on the outskirts of the city in small structures made of adobe (bricks of sun-dried earth and straw). Adobe homes were simple, handmade shelters that contained few luxuries. If an Aztec home contained any furniture at all, it was usually only a bed and some low tables. Reed mats were a common substitute for beds. Inside the home were a small courtyard and kitchen, as well as a family shrine to the gods. The bathroom was contained in a separate building that also housed a steam room where water was heated to create a spa-like environment. Bathing was a daily activity and was believed to contribute to a sense of spiritual and physical purification.

In traditional Aztec family life, the father was expected to provide shelter, food, and stability, while the mother raised the children and kept the home in order. The man of the house was also expected to work and pay a tribute to the king. Aztec children were often disciplined harshly by their parents; a common punishment was to be left outdoors overnight. Other punishments included scarring the skin with cactus needles or burning the skin with fire. While people today would consider this treatment abusive, such punishment was the norm in many Aztec families.

Most children were educated at free public schools, except for the children of nobility, who received private educations. Every child was educated in two separate institutions: the *Telpochcalli*, or House of Youth, and the *Cuicacalli*, an Aztec school for the arts. In the Telpochcalli, male students were taught martial arts, and female students were taught healing and domestic arts. At the Cuicacalli, both boys and girls were instructed in Aztec history, religion, customs, and arts such as singing, dancing, and playing musical instruments.

Aztec children attended school every single day from dawn until dusk. Sometimes they returned to school in the evening, after going home to bathe and change into ceremonial costumes that were worn for special events at the school. These ceremonies continued into the night, sometimes until midnight. In addition to their formal education, most children were instructed from a very early age in the tasks or trades that their parents felt were the best choices for their future livelihoods.

This is the Stone of the Sun, which the Aztecs used as a calendar.

The Aztecs divided their history into five ages known as suns. Each referred to a past world inhabited by Aztec ancestors who were destroyed by a god's rage, through fire, animal attacks, wind, or flood. The Aztecs believed that they lived in the age of the fifth sun, depicted by the *haab's* (calendar's) central image of Tonatiuh, the sun deity.

BELIEFS

The Aztecs were religious and explained their existence through creation and ancestral legends that they told and retold, keeping alive the stories of their origins, migration, and empire building. One of these legends describes the hardship endured by their ancestors, the Chichimecs, when they traveled across a vast and barren landscape in search of fertile land. Other stories explain the origin of the world and the Aztecs' place within it. These stories are also found on Aztec calendar stones that explain the Aztec conception of the universe.

Because they were so fearful of the gods and their potential rage, Aztecs constantly sacrificed people to satisfy and appease the gods. They believed that if the sun god were not fed human hearts and blood, the sun would not rise and the world—or fifth sun—would end in a disastrous earthquake. Their purpose in life was to delay that destruction for as long as possible. As a result of these beliefs, thousands of people were sacrificed to soothe the gods' wrath. Being sacrificed to the gods was considered a noble way to die—a service to one's nation—and it was said to guarantee admission to a higher level of heaven. For this reason, a surprising number of people were willing to lie upon a stone platform and have their hearts removed by Aztec priests.

Most Mesoamerican religious beliefs, including those of the Aztecs, conceived of existence as three separate levels of life: an overworld (a heaven or celestial space of thirteen levels), a middleworld (the earth inhabited by the living), and an underworld (sometimes referred to as *Mictlan*, or the "Place of the Dead," composed of nine levels). As is the case with other ancient civilizations, such as the Vikings, Aztecs believed that a colossal "tree of life" joined all three levels—the roots formed the underworld, the trunk was the middleworld, while the branches reached high into the overworld.

The Aztecs believed that the way they died, rather than the way they lived, would dictate how their spirits were treated in the afterlife. For example, if a woman died during childbirth, she would be guaranteed entry into one of heaven's highest levels, and the same would be true of a warrior who died in battle. If, by contrast, a person died of natural causes, he or she would have to pass through the nine levels of the underworld before reaching Mictlan, a process that was thought to take four years to complete.

WARFARE

The art of warfare was taught to young boys almost from birth, because Aztecs believed that their one purpose in life was to serve the gods. One of the best ways to serve them was to die for them (as we have seen in the case of human sacrifice). Yet Aztecs did not fight to the death, which they considered a clumsy and evil practice; instead, they fought to the point of capture using swords, knives, and shields. Captured warriors then would be prepared for ritual sacrifice to the gods. A "flowery death," as death following combat was known, was thought to earn men a high place in the heavens and undying respect on Earth. When Aztec warriors were not

This Aztec shield is decorated with a feather mosaic.

This is a reenactment of a warrior dance, one of only three traditional Aztec dances still performed today.

the purity of the Aztec army by removing any warriors who were not courageous enough.

A priest would usually lead soldiers into battle. Conflicts tended to be brief, usually lasting from dawn until dusk, or several days at most. They were fought in relay teams of twenty men, drawn from larger subdivisions of 200 to 400 warriors. And, although the battles were preceded by an eerie silence, the sounds of screams, drums, and whistles were heard at the outbreak of hostilities.

The Aztecs never surprised their enemies with sneak attacks. Instead, warriors first visited the enemy to warn them of the planned attack. They offered to call off the battle if the enemy agreed to pay the Aztecs tribute and submit to their rule. The enemy ruler of the foreign land had twenty days to decide whether to surrender and pay tribute or go to war. If he chose to fight, he risked the capture and ritual sacrifice of his people.

When the winning Aztec army returned home, the roadways were lined with flowers and the smell of burning incense filled the air. Massive celebrations began as the people rejoiced that a supply of sacrificial victims had been secured and the gods would be appeased for a little while longer.

defending their territory against foreign intruders or fighting to expand the empire, "flower wars" were organized with tribes from nearby cities to maintain a steady supply of sacrificial victims.

Since Aztecs emphasized the importance of meeting death bravely, willingly, and even enthusiastically, a show of fear while fighting was akin to treason and could result in execution. This punishment was meant to ensure

LANGUAGE

The Aztecs had a spoken language, called Nahuatl, but wrote only with glyphs, or picture characters, that were either inscribed or painted on pottery or on paper made from the bark of trees. The Nahuatl language often relied upon the use of extended metaphor for expression, a tendency that lent itself well to poetry. The Aztecs memorized and recited long passages of poetry, allowing them to transmit their history and religion from generation to generation. Many of the poems had rhythms that also encouraged speech and storytelling.

Official governmental and clerical information was often recorded using glyph characters (such as markings that indicated if and when an Aztec family had paid their tribute to the king). Other information written in glyphs included the Aztec calendar, episodes in Aztec history, and documents about the division of lands and the state of the population, which, at its height, grew to more than 12 million people. After the Spanish, led by Hernán Cortés, arrived from Cuba in 1519 and defeated the Aztecs in 1521, many original Aztec documents, called codices, were translated into Spanish.

Christian missionaries destroyed most Aztec libraries and their contents after the Spanish invasions. As a result, very few Aztec codices have been preserved.

ART

The Aztecs' artistic abilities are demonstrated by the wide range of beautiful artifacts that remain, ranging from pottery and codices to temples and pyramids. Their ingenuity is also attested to by the large array of materials—such as clay, feathers, stone, bone, seashells, and cloth—they skillfully used to create mosaic masks, headdresses, jewelry, dolls, helmets, and stone sculptures. A large portion of the population was highly skilled in many areas of craftmaking, and the Aztec culture and economy thrived as a result. The Aztec desire to create beautiful environments that were also engineering marvels is still observable today in the floating gardens and temples that remain standing, unharmed by the passage of time. Though the Aztecs' worst fears were realized and their world came to an end when the Spanish invaded their land, spread diseases, and defeated their warriors, stunning examples of their creative energy still exist today.

Warfare

Aztecs did not believe in killing their enemies during combat. Always intent on maintaining a supply of victims for sacrifice to the gods, they instead tried to capture their enemies on the battlefield. In fact, many battles were fought for no purpose other than gaining bodies for human sacrifice.

Occasionally, however, Aztecs went to war in order to gain more territory and increase the size of their empire. In such cases, Aztec warriors, clad in fighting gear, would visit the leader of the desired territory and demand the payment of a tribute to the Aztec emperor and surrender to his rule. The enemy was given a set time period in which to pay the tribute, normally twenty days, while the Aztecs inspected the foreign land and planned a battle strategy based on their observations. If the tribute was not paid, the warriors would capture the land and its people, who would then be prepared for sacrifice.

This Aztec relief depicts two warriors in battle, clad in feathered helmets and bearing swords and shields.

According to accounts by Spanish soldiers, the Aztecs were fierce fighters who maintained a strict discipline, remained in orderly formations and, as a group, were very colorful and handsome. The Aztecs wore no armor or coat of mail; instead, they soaked their clothing in a salt solution that made the fabric stiff and less vulnerable to sharp blades. Although this seems like scant protection against spears and knives, their clothing was also quilted, the body protected under layers of thick material. The Aztecs also wore wooden helmets that were covered in colorful feathers and shaped like animal heads.

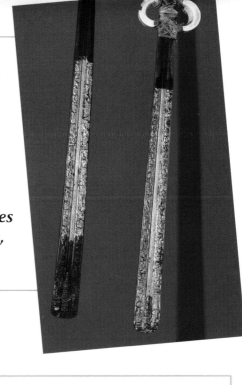

One of the most important pieces of the Aztec warrior's equipment was his atlatl, *or spear thrower. The two shown here are carved with scenes of gods, warriors, and sacrifice.*

Aztec warriors were characterized by their colorful attire, which indicated their social position and combat experience. For instance, young warriors who had not been in many battles, and therefore had captured few prisoners, wore their own clothing and carried a simple shield (made of woven reeds and feathers) and a spear called an *atlatl.* Sometimes, wooden clubs were used for fighting in close combat. Veteran warriors adopted attire that indicated their rank and experience, including special headdresses and insignia. In addition, distinctions were made between warriors of different social classes. The *pipiltin* (warriors from the noble class) wore feathered suits, while warriors from the *macehualtin* (commoners) wore suits of animal skin.

Aztec warriors were often identified by their battle gear. This is one of Montezuma's noble fighters.

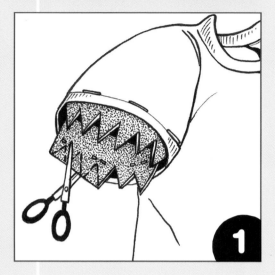

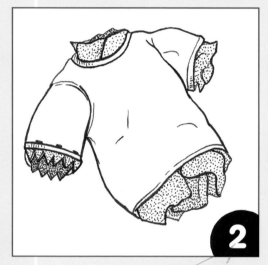

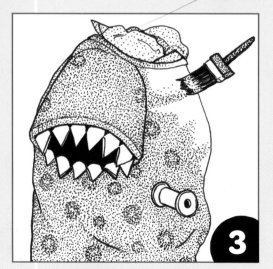

Warrior Helmet

Make a warrior's headdress like the ones worn by soldiers in Montezuma's army.

YOU WLL NEED
- T-shirt
- Felt or fabric scraps
- Newspaper
- Cardboard
- Paper fasteners
- Craft paint
- Pencil
- Thread spool
- Feathers or fur
- Needle and thread

Step 1
Cut two pieces of cardboard to approximately the size of the T-shirt sleeves. Make the ends jagged. These are your animal's teeth. Set the cardboard pieces in the sleeve opening of the T-shirt "helmet," like a visor. Staple them in place along the sleeve's cuff, as shown.

Step 2
Stuff the T-shirt with crumpled newspapers. This will act as a structural support while you are making your helmet.

Step 3
Paint the entire T-shirt any color. Allow it to dry. The paint will make the fabric firm. Paint details such as leopard spots by using a thread spool as a stamp.

Step 4
With scraps of fabric, cut out half-circle ear shapes. Use the needle and thread to sew them to the top of your helmet.

Step 5
Paint facial features, such as eyes, brows, and nostrils, on the helmet's animal head. Paint its cardboard teeth white.

Step 6
Add details such as a feather crown by cutting or ripping strips of fabric and attaching them with safety pins along the collar of the T-shirt, as shown. Remove the paper stuffing and try it on!

Rituals and Celebrations

The "new fire" ceremony was the most important of all the Aztec rituals. It marked the end of one fifty-two-year cycle and the beginning of another (similar to the importance we attach to the turning of a millennium). It was thought that a new fire had to be lit in order to embark successfully upon the next fifty-two-year cycle. If a fire was not lit, Aztecs feared that the sun would be extinguished and the world would end.

In the weeks before the ceremony took place, people throughout the entire city extinguished their home fires in preparation for the arrival of the new flame. At sunset, to begin the ceremony, priests climbed to a temple on the top of an extinct volcanic crater called the Hill of the Star. The "new fire" was started in the cut-open chest of a sacrificial victim. After the fire was successfully lit, all of the altars in the temples throughout the empire could be lit again using flames from this new fire. If anyone wanted to please the gods during the ceremony, they would cut themselves and sprinkle

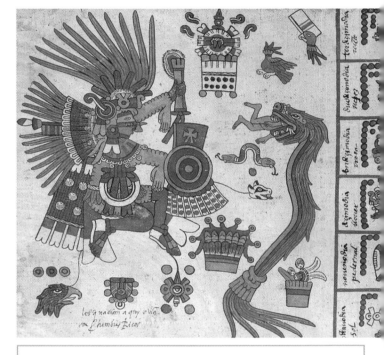

This is an image of the feathered serpent Quetzalcoatl, god of art, and Tezcatlipoca, god of the night sky. Tezcatlipoca often disguised himself as a jaguar; his spotted skin was compared to the starry sky.

the blood in the direction of the new fire. Afterward, the flames were taken down the mountain and carried to the pyramid temple of Huitzilopochtli in the center of the city. Everyone took part in the ceremony by carrying a flame from this central fire into their home.

In all, there were more than 300 Aztec festivals, rituals, and ceremonies each year. By participating in so many religious observances, Aztec society became more united and communal, and therefore easier for the king to rule. Above all, the Aztecs felt these ceremonies appeased the gods and kept chaos and destruction at bay.

Priests often dressed as gods during rituals and ceremonies, and wore elaborate masks made of tiny turquoise mosaics. Many of these masks are thought to depict the fire god, Xiuhtecuhtli; the god of rain and fertility, Tlaloc; and the god of art, Quetzalcoatl, also known as the Feathered Serpent. Other materials for masks included seashells, bone, and semiprecious stones, all of which were glued with beeswax to human skulls that had the back portion of the cranium removed.

Modern Mexicans sometimes practice the traditional rituals of their Aztec ancestors, such as the fire dance.

This pre-Columbian Aztec mask was made of a human skull covered with bits of turquoise.

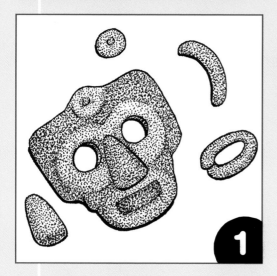

Mosaic Mask

Perform your own ritual of celebration and dance around your room wearing your very own Aztec mask, similar in design to the very artifacts that were found buried inside the Great Temple.

YOU WILL NEED
- Modeling clay
- White glue and water (for papier-mâché paste)
- Large bowl and spoon
- Newspaper
- Colorful magazine pages
- Clear varnish or acrylic gloss medium
- Scissors
- Hole puncher

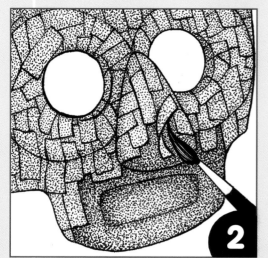

Step 1
Begin your mask by making a base with modeling clay. Flatten a large amount of clay and shape it into a circle. Squeeze the bottom of the circle to make a jaw. Next, roll a small lump of clay to make a nose. Make holes for eyes, or add eyes later.

Step 2
When you are satisfied with your mask shape, make a papier-mâché paste by mixing water and white glue in a large bowl (three parts glue to one part water). Rip small pieces of newspaper into strips. Dip the strips into the paste and cover your clay form with six to eight layers of glued paper, allowing drying time between layers.

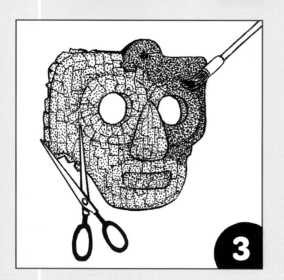

Step 3
Once the mask has completely dried remove the clay from the interior. Trim the edge of your mask with scissors if you desire a smoother appearance.

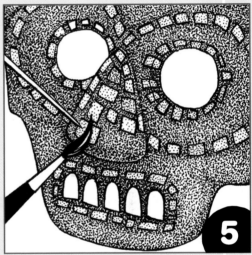

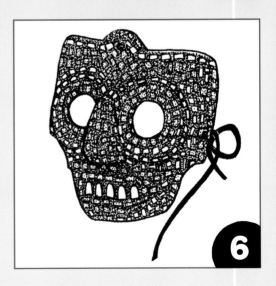

Step 4
Paint your mask a solid dark color such as blue. While the paint is drying, cut magazine pages into tiny tiles.

Step 5
Apply the tiles to the mask with the glue and water solution and a paintbrush. Use tiles of the same color to outline the eyes. If you want, use a tooth-pick to help position the paper squares while you attach them.

Step 6
Cut pieces of white paper to make teeth and glue them to the mask's mouth. Once your mosaic is complete, allow it to dry. You can punch holes in its sides to tie strings for wearing on your face or hanging on your wall. Finally, cover the entire mask with a coat of clear varnish or clear acrylic gloss medium.

Religion and Beliefs

The people of Mexica worshiped many gods on a daily basis. According to their earliest beliefs, two gods named Ometecuhtli and Omecihuatl created the universe. These gods were known as the "Lord and Lady of Duality." Over time, the Aztecs added more gods to their religion, some drawn from the legends of their ancient ancestors and some from surrounding cultures. Most of these gods were associated with the earth or sky—with fertility, agriculture, and the wider universe.

As we have seen, human sacrifice formed the core of Aztec religion. It was believed that blood sacrifice would perpetuate Aztec civilization. An Aztec legend described the making of the fifth sun (the fifth Aztec world or era). The legend stated that the sun could not be created until one of the gods volunteered to leap into the fire and be destroyed.

Many sacrifices, especially those involving defeated enemies, incorporated cannibalism. After the victim's heart was removed, Aztec priests would consume the flesh of his or her arms and legs.

In this image of an Aztec sacrifice, a priest raises a small sword before using it to remove the victim's heart.

These rituals were attended by large groups of people who would wait for the body of the victim to be thrown down the stairs of the temple. Afterward, the heart was placed in a chacmool statue (a sculpture of a reclining figure holding a bowl that would contain the heart) as a tribute to the gods. According to some accounts, some 20,000 people were sacrificed in one day by Aztec priests, who were described by the Spanish as frightening creatures. They wore black cloaks, had long fingernails, and black hair matted with dried blood. They reeked of death and their ears were scarred and cut as a form of penance, or self-punishment.

This illustration from a codex depicts Aztecs killing someone as a sacrifice to the sun.

The Aztecs were so anxious to prevent the destructive wrath of the gods that they were often very watchful of any bad omens, or signs of divine displeasure. Only ten years before the Spanish invaded Mexico, the Aztecs were said to have been visited by a series of ominous signs that included flames in the sky and violent ocean waves. Smallpox, which was also taken as a sign of their impending doom, was brought to the New World by Europeans. This terrible disease reached epidemic proportions in the sixteenth century and devastated the Aztec population.

This Aztec knife was most likely used for human sacrifices.

This chacmool statue was found in the ruins of the Aztec Templo Mayor, Tenochtitlán, in modern-day Mexico City.

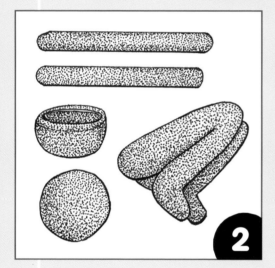

Chacmool Statue

Sculpt an Aztec chacmool statue just like the one sitting outside Templo Mayor in what was the ancient city of Tenochtitlán.

YOU WILL NEED
- **Sawdust clay**
- **Toothpick**
- **Aluminum foil**
- **Baking sheet**

Sawdust Clay Recipe
1 cup sawdust
1/2 cup cornstarch
1 teaspoon powdered alum
3/4 cup hot water

Mix the sawdust, cornstarch, and alum together in a large saucepan. Gradually add the water and stir until well mixed. Cook over low heat for about five minutes while stirring constantly. Remove from heat and place on a foil-lined baking sheet. Allow the clay to cool slightly before using.

Step 1
Make the sawdust clay using the recipe on this page. When your clay is cool enough to handle, roll a lump of it into a ball. This will form the head of your chacmool statue.

Step 2
Roll small lumps of clay into tubes for the arms and legs, and roll a small ball for the sacrifice container that the chacmool will hold.

Step 3
Take the remaining clay and roll it into a tube for the body. To create a base for the statue, spread the clay at the bottom of the body outward, so that the bottom is wider than the body itself. Attach the head and limbs to the body, as shown.

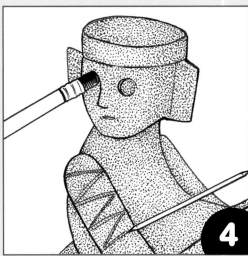

Step 4
Sculpt a face on the chacmool using a pencil. Make lines in the arms and across the body to represent the figure's gown and jewelry.

Step 5
Attach the small sacrificial container to the hands of the chacmool and add decorative details with a toothpick. When your sculpture is complete, set it in a sunny window for a few days to fully dry. Remember to turn the sculpture on its side so that the bottom will also dry.

Step 6
You can leave your chacmool in its natural state or give it color by making some homemade paint using the following directions:

- **Red** Cut beets into small pieces. Cook on medium heat for thirty minutes with distilled water. Strain the juice into a jar or cup when cool.
- **Blue** Cook blueberries in distilled water over medium heat for thirty minutes. Strain into a cup or jar when cool.
- **Brown**   Add 1 tablespoon of instant coffee to 2 tablespoons of hot water. Mix and let cool.

Writing and Literature

The Aztecs created a system of writing using glyphs, in which a picture or symbol represented a specific word or idea. These glyphs often appeared in books, or codices, which are paper documents folded like an accordion and painted with complex images and signs. Glyphs could also be found on pottery, on the walls of temples, and on sculptures, such as the coronation stones marking a king's reign.

Scribes worked exclusively with a rough paper called *amatl* made from the bark of mulberry and wild fig trees. A scribe, who was considered noble, worked in the service of the king and was well educated and highly skilled. He was also a trained painter who used pigments created from soot and plant dyes.

This fresco depicts Aztec painters and scribes at work.

Scribes also designed codices, most of which have perished. But some translations created after the Spanish defeated the Aztecs in 1521 have remained. For instance, a thirteen-volume book written by Father Bernadino de Sahagun in 1529, called the *Florentine Codex* (codex is the singular form of codices), or the *General History of the Things in New Spain*, details some aspects of Aztec life. Some of the translated codices included governmental information, such as population counts, tax records, and calendars, while others recorded religious events and ceremonies.

This relief sculpture from Xochicalco is written in the Nahuatl language.

The most famous Aztec codex of all is the *Mendoza Codex*, which contains a great deal of information about how the Aztecs lived. It describes scenes from daily life and includes illustrations of Aztec costumes, jewelry, and musical instruments. The codex was commissioned by the Spanish governor Antonio de Mendoza, who wanted a detailed record of sixteenth-century family life in Mexico. One legend states, however, that it was a gift to the king of Spain and was therefore protected from the fiery fate that most Aztec codices met at the hands of Christian missionaries.

This Mexican codex shows the genealogy of the Aztec civilization.

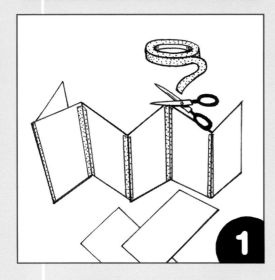

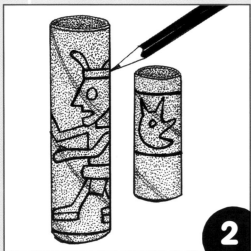

Codex

Pretend you are an Aztec scribe and paint a codex. Include bright and beautiful pictures and symbols.

YOU WILL NEED
- **Thick paper or oak tag**
- **Pencil**
- **Masking tape**
- **White glue**
- **Cardboard toilet paper and paper towel tubes**
- **String or yarn**
- **Craft paint**
- **Large paint brush**

Step 1
To make your codex book, tape several pieces of paper together along their vertical edges, as shown.

Step 2
Draw figures and symbols along the width of a cardboard tube. Leave a one-inch border at both ends. Look at images in this book to get ideas for Aztec figures and symbols. Make the lines of your drawings as thick as the string or yarn you have available. You can vary your design by creating more than one tube. Additional tubes could be of varying sizes, such as a roll from toilet tissue.

Step 3
In small sections, trace over your design with white glue. Set pieces of string into the glue. Use a toothpick to nudge the string pieces exactly where you want them. These tubes will function as stamp rollers.

Step 4
When the glued strings have fully dried, paint the surface of your tubes (but not the one-inch borders at either end) with a large brush and craft paint. Coat the entire tube with water using a dampened brush.

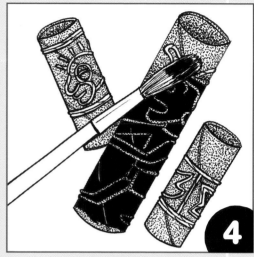

Step 5
While holding the unpainted ends of the tube, gently roll it onto the paper codex to make a print. You can reuse your tube stamp many times.

Step 6
When the paint has fully dried, you can add colorful detail to your codex by painting in some or all of the designs you have printed.

Art and Architecture

All of the Mesoamerican peoples built temples dedicated to their gods. One of the greatest temple structures ever built by the Aztecs was erected at the heart of the city of Tenochtitlán on the supposed site of the god Huitzilopochtli's birthplace (Huitzilopochtli is the Aztec god of war). Behind a great wall that separated the temple from the city, steps ascended to two shrines, one dedicated to the rain god Tlaloc, the other to Huitzilopochtli. The Great Temple was the spiritual center of the Aztec world and the place where all sacrifices—both animal and human—took place.

The Great Temple actually began as a small, primitive shrine. Because the Aztecs held the gods in such high esteem, more and more temples were built around and on top of the original building. Eventually, the complex grew to a height of over 100 feet. Though only about one-fifth the height of the Great Pyramid at Giza in Egypt, it allowed an impressive view of the city. Outside the Great Temple, racks of human skulls were aligned in rows, creating an altar called *tzompantlis*. It represented the lives of those sacrificed in order to please the gods. It was widely believed that the skulls also insured the continued safety and prosperity of the entire civilization.

The oldest, innermost chamber of the Great Temple complex featured a sacrificial altar and a chacmool—a statue that held the hearts and the blood of those who had been sacrificed to the gods. After the heart of the sacrificed person or animal was removed, the bodies were then thrown down from the top of the temple's massive steps, leaving a bloody trail that would remain for all to see. Everyone gathered to watch the human sacrifices; the victims often were slaves or prisoners of war. The sacrificial rituals were elaborate. Servants performed certain tasks, such as washing a victim's feet or dressing him or her in ceremonial attire.

Many gifts were placed before the statue of Huitzilopochtli, such as gems and objects made of gold and silver. Eventually, the Great Temple was torn down piece by piece and used by Catholic missionaries to create a Spanish cathedral. Hernán Cortés built his own home on top of Montezuma's palace. By 1692, nearly all of the Aztec art was completely destroyed. Upon excavation of the Great Temple, archaeologists found more than 6,000 objects buried inside some of the temples that were offerings to the gods.

The Metropolitan Cathedral stands in Mexico City's main square, the Zocalo. It is the former site of the Aztec Great Temple, or Templo Mayor, which was torn down in 1524 by Spanish invaders.

This restored Aztec temple pyramid is in the present-day town of Santa Cecilia Acatitlan, just north of Mexico City, Mexico.

1

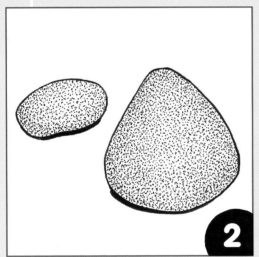

2

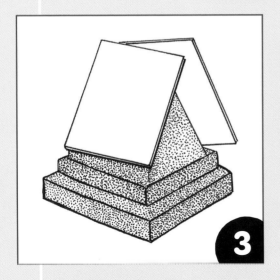

3

The Great Temple

Build your very own stairway to the sky and recreate a majestic Aztec temple.

YOU WILL NEED
- **Sand clay**
- **2 five-inch square pieces of cardboard**
- **Craft knife**
- **Toothpicks**
- **Ruler**
- **Saucepan**

Sand Clay Recipe
3 cups sand (beach or play sand)
1 1/2 cups cornstarch
3 teaspoons powdered alum
2 1/2 cups hot water

Combine all dry ingredients in a saucepan. Add water and cook over low heat. Mix continuously for about five minutes, or until the mixture is thick. Remove from heat. Pour the mixture onto your work surface. Allow it to cool for several minutes before kneading.

Step 1
Mix a batch of sand clay following the recipe on this page.

Step 2
Set aside a large handful of the sand clay. Roll the rest into a ball. Then form the ball into a cone shape

Step 3
Using two pieces of cardboard, apply pressure to the opposite sides of the cone using the straight edges of the cardboard as a guide. Repeat this on the opposite sides. Continue until all four sides are the same, like a pyramid. Next, create "steps" in your pyramid by pressing the sides one-half inch from the bottom. Next, move up another one-half inch and press in the sides again. Continue until you reach the top.

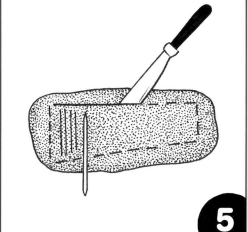

Step 4

Cut the tip of your pyramid with a blunt craft knife and flatten the surface. Moisten your fingers with tap water and smooth the pyramid's angles of any bumps. With some of the remaining clay, make two small pyramids to serve as the shrines at the top of your temple and attach them by smoothing the edges of their bases onto the top of the main pyramid.

Step 5

Roll a piece of clay into a tube and flatten it evenly. Cut out a rectangular piece of clay and attach it to the front of the temple to make the stairway. Use a knife or toothpicks to add decorative details, like stairs, for your temple.

Step 6

Place the temple model in a sunny window to dry. This may take a few days, depending on the room temperature. After the temple dries, lay it on its side so that the bottom will also dry.

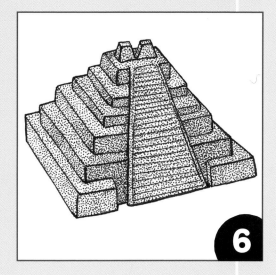

Aztec Craftspeople

The Aztecs were skilled artisans who worked with many natural materials such as clay, stone, human and animal bones, plants, feathers, seashells, and hand-woven cloth. They were resourceful and used the materials available to them in highly creative ways.

Paper was derived from the bark of mulberry and wild fig trees. It was soaked and divided into sheets and coated with a chalky substance. The strips were long, so after they dried, scribes divided and folded them into the characteristic accordion design that we find in many Aztec codices.

Fabric and thread were made from the fibers of the maguey plant, a common species of cactus that grows in Mexico. Most Aztecs wore clothing derived from this plant. Only wealthy men were permitted to wear cotton, which was very expensive and grown in the warmer, lower valleys.

This handmade textile was found at Templo Mayor, inside an Aztec offering to Tlaloc, the god of rain.

Clay, which was dug from the earth, was shaped by hand (the Aztecs didn't use potters' wheels) and was hardened in the hot sun. Sun bricks were made using the same method. Stone masonry was also a popular Aztec art, and one of the oldest. Huge blocks of stone were positioned and carved to create temples and statues, as well as small household idols for personal worship. Obsidian, a hard, volcanic rock, was a common material used to make "smoking mirrors."

According to legend, Aztec priests would gaze into the mirror and see clouds of smoke that would eventually part to show a vision of future events. Since obsidian could be sharpened to a point, it was also used to make knives and weapons.

Aztecs who worked the land or had a skill were known as *mace-hualtin*. This class of people also included artisans, such as cloth dyers, jewelers, potters, scribes, and stone and metal workers. The craftspeople would carry their wares to local marketplaces where excess goods were traded or paid for with cacao beans (from which chocolate, cocoa, and cocoa butter are made). More often than not, these individuals passed their skills on to their children who became their apprentices. For instance, from a young age most girls were taught by their mothers how to spin thread and weave cloth using a simple loom.

This pottery dish was probably used ceremonially. It is decorated with skulls. Skull imagery was used to symbolize death and rebirth, and to honor the dead.

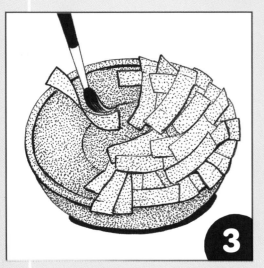

Aztec Bowl

Just as the Aztecs crafted pottery by hand, you too can practice this ancient craft.

YOU WILL NEED
- White glue
- Water
- Newspaper
- Scissors
- Petroleum jelly or liquid soap
- Small glass or plastic bowl
- Cardboard
- Masking tape
- Craft paint
- Acrylic gloss or shellac (optional)

Step 1
Make papier-mâché paste by combining three parts glue with one part water in a bowl.

Step 2
Find a small glass or plastic bowl to use as a mold. Coat its interior with a layer of petroleum jelly or liquid soap so the papier-mâché will not stick to it when it dries.

Step 3
Tear strips of newspaper into small pieces. Cover the interior of the bowl with six to eight layers of newspaper dipped into the paste. Allow it to dry overnight.

Step 4
When the newspaper has completely dried and hardened, remove it from the bowl. Trim the edges of your papier-mâché bowl if you desire, or leave it uneven for a more ragged effect.

Step 5

Cut a strip from a piece of cardboard. The strip should be as wide as the desired height of your bowl's base. Attach the ends of the strip together with a piece of tape to make a circular band. Use a few pieces of tape to attach the band to the bottom of the bowl. Cover the circular band and the tape with two layers of papier-mâché. Allow it to dry.

Step 6

Paint your bowl with craft paint. Look at other pictures in this book to get ideas for various designs. When your paint is dry, you can apply a coat of acrylic gloss or shellac to give it a shiny finish.

Decorative Arts

As in many civilizations past and present, jewelry and clothing worn by members of Aztec society were symbols of their wealth and power.

A person's place in society usually dictated what he or she was allowed to wear. The Aztecs considered it a crime for someone to wear clothing that was too elaborate or fancy for his or her position. Most clothing was very simple, loose, and flowing, often not more than a piece of material draped around part of the body. For example, men often wore loincloths, while Aztec women normally wore skirts wrapped around their hips. Commoners had to wear shorter lengths of fabric, while longer, elaborately trimmed garments were reserved for kings and other nobles. The nobility wore brightly colored cotton fabrics, jeweled collars made of precious stones, and flattened gold jewelry in their ears

This painting illustrates the strict social ranks of the Aztecs.

and noses. They also had magnificent ceremonial costumes reserved for religious rituals and war. Ceremonial costumes were commonly made of fur, animal skins, feathers, gold and silver pieces, and strips of painted leather. Patterns woven into clothing had symbolic meaning, such as geometric designs that represented the earth and sky.

The wearing of fine jewelry was restricted to the nobility. Even jewelry made of common materials, such as seashells, could not be worn by just anyone. Although few could actually wear them, the Aztecs made jewelry out of gold and silver and small fragments of precious and semiprecious stones, such as jade and crystal.

Even hairstyles were an expression of a person's status in Aztec society. Their hair was coarse, black, and straight. Men usually wore it cut in a fringe over the forehead and allowed the rest to grow almost shoulder length. The priests had their own distinctive hair style, and the warriors wore pigtails and created various kinds of hair ridges to indicate how many prisoners they had captured. Male facial hair was considered unpleasant, and mothers applied hot cloths to their sons' faces to prevent hair growth.

Women let their hair grow long. Most single women allowed their hair to hang loose to the waist, but on festival days it was braided with ribbons. Married women typically wore their hair in two braids, which were twisted around the head with the ends sticking up like two little horns above the eyebrows.

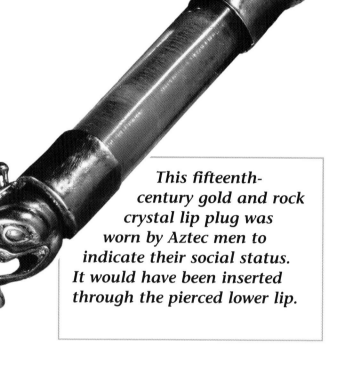

This fifteenth-century gold and rock crystal lip plug was worn by Aztec men to indicate their social status. It would have been inserted through the pierced lower lip.

An Aztec necklace

Beaded Jewelry

Pretend you are Aztec nobility by making your own golden and beaded jewelry.

YOU WILL NEED
- Colorful magazine pages
- White glue
- Pencil
- Scissors
- String
- Darning needle

Step 1
Cut magazine pages into long strips. Use the most colorful pages you can find from unwanted magazines.

Step 2
Dip each strip into white glue. Wrap the glued strip around the end of a pencil. Slip the rolled paper from the pencil and allow it to dry. This is your first bead; make many more in assorted sizes and colors.

Step 3
Once your beads have dried, they are ready to be strung into necklaces or bracelets.

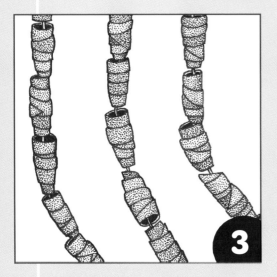

Step 4
To make jewelry in the style of an Aztec shell necklace, use a darning needle to carefully make holes through the width of your beads, and string them together.

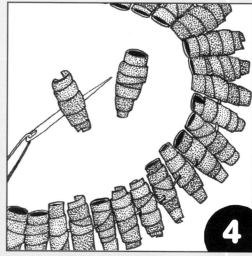

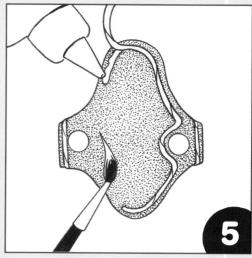

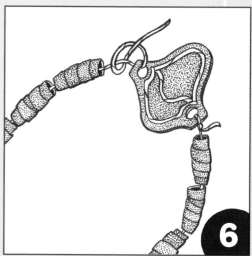

Step 5
To make a decorative clasp for your jewelry, cut a small piece of cardboard into a shape, such as an animal or human. Make two holes on each side of the clasp. Decorate the clasp with glued pieces of string and paint.

Step 6
Tie the ends of the strings through the holes of the clasp. If you desire, make bracelets and necklaces of multiple strands using this same method.

Leisure and Play

Although the Aztecs spent much of their time working, leisure activities were also important, especially in connection with their many rituals, festivals, and celebrations. Most of these occasions demanded that people dance to music that was played on clay pipes, cane panpipes, gourd rattles, whistles, and flutes. Drums, such as the long and narrow *teponaztli* and the *huehuetl*, were used frequently, too. Although dancing and music were seen as leisure activities, in many cases they served a very serious purpose and played an important part in religious ceremonies. Even sporting events revolved around the worship of the Aztec gods.

Yet Aztecs did know how to play just for the fun of it. One common Aztec game was *patolli*, a board game similar to Parcheesi. Players tossed beans

This colorful illustration was taken from a codex. It shows children playing the ancient game of patolli.

instead of dice, and game pieces were made from naturally colored or red and blue painted stones. Aztecs played patolli to win valuables such as jewelry, including golden necklaces, turquoise bracelets, quetzal feathers, and green stone earrings.

The Aztecs enjoyed gambling on games like patolli, and people could wager almost anything they owned, including their homes, farms, and occasionally, their slaves and children. These gambling matches often drew large crowds of onlookers who would sometimes place bets on who the likely winner would be.

Another Aztec game was called *ulama*, or *ollamaliztli*. It was similar to our game of basketball, but the stakes were much higher than they were in a game of patolli. Two teams of between one and six players tried to bounce a small ball off their hips through a ring in order to score points on a court designed specifically for this purpose. Only Aztecs of nobility could play ulama, however, and often the losers were killed as a sacrifice to the gods.

Children almost never had time to play, but younger children who could not yet work or attend school played in and around their homes. Some early pull toys with wheels have been found by archaeologists, despite the fact that Aztecs never used the wheel for any practical purposes, such as on wagons or carts.

Small girls played with dolls that they may have woven themselves, in order to practice the craft. They were often buried with these dolls after they died; the only surviving Aztec dolls have been found in coffins.

This ring hangs above a ball court. The Aztecs played a game similar to basketball.

This teponaztli, *a two-toned drum, has an owl carved on its side.*

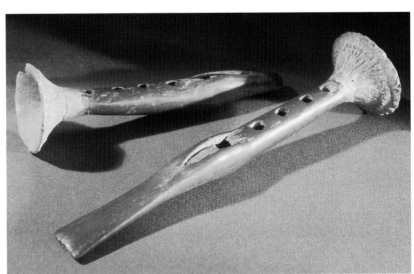

These are typical Aztec flageolets, *or small flutes.*

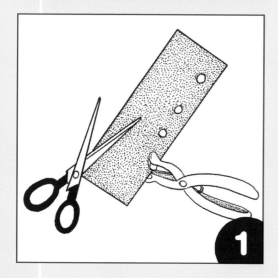

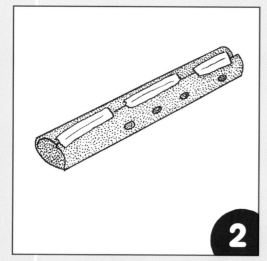

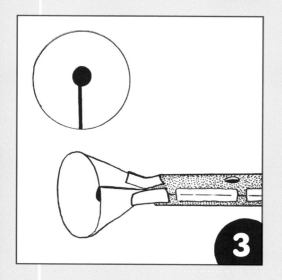

Aztec Flute

Pretend to play your own music, just like the Mexica did, with this flute that dates to the height of the Aztec civilization.

YOU WILL NEED
- Cardboard scraps
- Masking tape
- Hole puncher
- White glue
- Water
- Newspaper
- Paintbrush
- Craft paint

Step 1
Cut a rectangle out of a scrap piece of cardboard, approximately 8 inches by 2 1/2 inches. Using a hole puncher, carefully punch several holes down the length of one side, spacing them equally.

Step 2
Roll the cardboard rectangle into a tube shape with the punched holes facing the top. Tape it together along its seam.

Step 3
Next, using another piece of scrap cardboard, cut out a circle, approximately 5 inches in circumference. Cut through half of it to its center point. Then, gently twist it into a cone shape. Close the opening with masking tape. Using more tape, attach the taped cone shape to the end of the cardboard tube made in step 2.

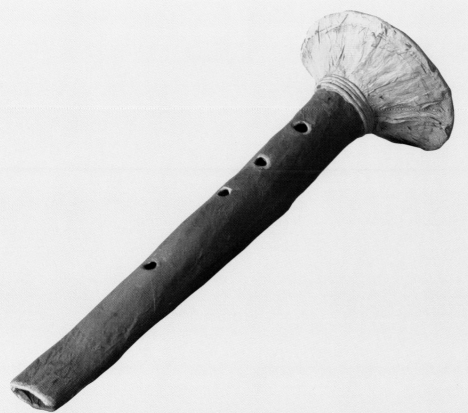

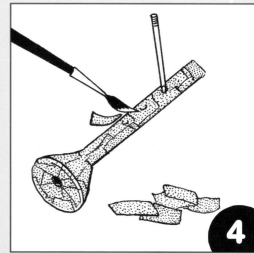

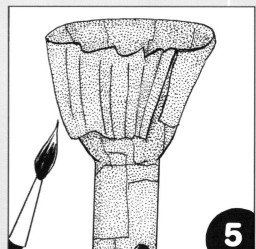

Step 4

When your instrument seems sturdy, cover it with three layers of papier-mâché. To do this, dip small bits of newspaper into a water and glue solution (one part water to three parts glue) and attach them to the instrument, covering the entire flute except the fingering holes. Set aside to dry between layers.

Step 5

To create a texture on the rounded end of your instrument, pleat the wet papier-mâché to form evenly spaced lines with your fingers. You can also achieve a satisfactory textured effect by tightly crumpling newspaper bits before attaching them.

Step 6

After your instrument has completely dried, paint it any color you desire.

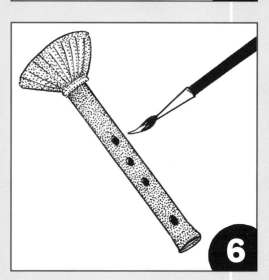

TIMELINE

BC	**5000**	Maize (corn) grows in Mexico.
	3500	Egyptians develop first hieroglyphs.
	3372	First date on Mayan calendar.
	3100	Sumerians invent a system of writing. Upper and Lower Egypt are united.
	2650	Egyptians build step pyramid for King Zoser.
	2575	Egypt's Old Kingdom begins. Construction begins on the Great Pyramids and the Sphinx in Giza.
	1650	Mycenaean culture develops in Greece.
	1500	Stone temples appear in Mexico.
	1200	Olmec civilization develops in Mexico.
	776	First Olympic Games in Greece.
	449	Building of the Parthenon begins.
	336	Alexander the Great rules Greece.
	323	Alexander the Great dies. Greek Hellenistic period begins.
	300	Rise of Maya civilization in Mesoamerica.
	49	Julius Caesar rules Rome.
	30	Egypt becomes a Roman province.
AD	**5**	Approximate birth of Jesus in Bethlehem.
	43	Romans invade Britain.
	54	Nero becomes Rome's emperor and outlaws Christianity.
	72	Construction begins on the Colosseum in Rome.
	79	Mount Vesuvius destroys the Roman towns of Pompeii and Herculaneum.
	1200	The Chichimecs leave northern Mexico and head south toward present-day Mexico City.
	1325	The Chichimecs arrive in Mexico's central basin, found Tenochtitlán, and build the Aztec Empire.
	1519	The Spanish arrive in Mexico from Cuba.
	1520	The Spanish invade Tenochtitlán and take Montezuma hostage.
	1521	The Spanish destroy Tenochtitlán and the Aztec Empire falls soon after.

GLOSSARY

amatl   Type of paper made from tree bark.

archaeologist   Person who studies ancient civilizations by analyzing their objects.

artifact   Object, especially a tool, made by humans.

calmecac   Aztec temple school for the sons of nobles.

Chichimec   Nomadic ancestors of the Aztec people.

codex (plural codices)   Aztec book of picture symbols.

cuicacalli   School where Aztec children learned about the arts.

glyph   Picture symbol standing for a word or idea.

haab   Aztec sun calendar.

Huitzilopochtli   God of war and sun.

Mesoamerican   Describes people who lived in central and southern Mexico, Guatemala, and parts of El Salvador between 1000 BC and AD 1521.

Mexica   Area settled by Aztecs that later became Mexico.

Mictlan   Underworld of eternal darkness and emptiness where, according to Aztec legend, most people descended when they died.

mosaic   Decoration or picture made from tiny stones or glass.

patolli   Game played on a board with colored stones.

pyramid   A building with sloping sides and a square base.

sacrifice   To kill an animal or a person as an offering to a god.

scribe   Person who writes documents and books by hand.

telpochcalli   School for common Aztec boys.

tlachtli   Ball game played in ancient Mexico.

Tlaloc   God of rain and fertility.

tlatocan   Large council that advised Aztec kings.

Tonalpohualli   Sun god who rules the current age, according to Mexica legend; also an Aztec term for a 260-day calendar.

tribute   Tax paid in food and other goods.

underworld   Place where the Aztecs believed people went after death.

Xiuhtecuhtli   God of fire.

FOR MORE INFORMATION

ORGANIZATIONS

American Museum of Natural History
Central Park West at 79th Street
New York, NY 10024-5194
(212) 769-5100
Web Site: http://www.amnh.org

Archaeological Institute of America
Boston University
656 Beacon Street, 4th floor
Boston, MA 02215-2006
Web Site: http://www.archaeology.org

Boston Museum of Fine Arts
465 Huntington Avenue
Boston, MA 02115-5523
Web Site: http://www.mfa.org

Metropolition Museum of Art
1000 Fifth Avenue
New York, NY 10028
Web Site: http://www.metmuseum.org

Smithsonian Institution Information Center
1000 Jefferson Drive SW
Washington, DC 20560-0010
(202) 357-2700
Web Site: http://www.si.edu

World Archaeological Society
120 Lakewood Drive
Hollister, MO 65672

In Canada

Ontario Archaeological Society
11099 Bathhurst Street
Richmond Hill, ON L4C ON2
(905) 787-9851
Web site: http://www.ontarioarchaeology.on.ca

Royal Ontario Museum
100 Queen's Park
Toronto, ON M5S 2C6
Web site: http://www.rom.on.ca

WEB SITES

The Ancient Aztecs
http://library.thinkquest.org/27981

Dig: The Archaeology Magazine for Kids
http://www.digonsite.com

The History Channel.Com
http://www.historychannel.com

FOR FURTHER READING

Burr, Claudia. *What the Aztecs Told Me.*
    Berkeley, CA: Publishers Group West, 1997.
Hull, Robert. *The Aztecs.* Austin, TX: Raintree
    Steck-Vaughn, 1998.
Mason, Anthony. *Aztec Times.* New York:
    Simon & Schuster, 1997.
Steele, Philip. *The Aztec News.* Cambridge, MA:
    Candlewick Press, 1997.

INDEX

ABOUT THE AUTHOR AND ILLUSTRATOR

Joann Jovinelly and Jason Netelkos have been working together on one project or another for more than a decade. This is their first collaborative series for young readers. They live in New York City.

PHOTO CREDITS

SERIES DESIGN AND LAYOUT

Evelyn Horovicz